Anastasia was through making out with Ian. He was never going to change.

Suzanne marveled at the fact that she was still single. Well, at least she had her vintage Judy Blume collection to keep her company on those long winter nights.

"Ooooooooh!"

"Don't be fooled by the rock that I got. I'm still Penny, Penny from the block."

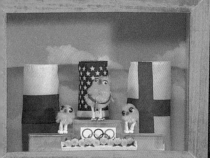
er@n

"For the love of God, man, stop calling me Twenty. The name's Nigel."

...e knew all about the dangers of UV rays... but ...ed, baked or fried, she just knew she looked her ...tan.

...d to ask herself if the 'all over' body wax had in fact ...bad idea.

At $150.00 a session, Amy didn't want to talk about her intimacy issues. She wanted to know what Dr. Arlow thought of her new shoes, if he liked the bangs and if he too looked forward to their weekly sessions with a gnawing anticipation?

Coco dreamed that one day she would grow up to be a benevolent queen... or a supermodel.

Abandoned once again in his padded basket, Icarus plotted a swift and su... revenge. "Sleep with one eye open Mother."

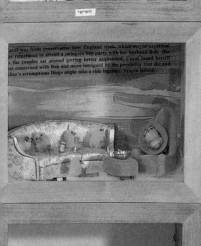
...arol was from conservative New England stock, which maybe explained ...er reluctance to attend a swingers hip party with her husband Bob. But ...s the couples sat around getting better acquainted, Carol found herself ...ss enamored with Bob and more intrigued by the possibility that she and ...lice's scrumptious Diego might take a ride together. Vroom indeed.

...a. Barbara and Flo had been sitting outside that soda fountain since ...6. If it happened to Lana, it could happen to them.

"You binge, I'll purge."

A penny here, a penny there. One day Vivica would save enough to ... her hair thermally reconditioned too.

BITTER WITH BAGGAGE SEEKS SAME

BITTER WITH BAGGAGE SEEKS SAME

THE LIFE AND TIMES OF SOME CHICKENS

Sloane Tanen

PHOTOGRAPHS BY STEFAN HAGEN

BLOOMSBURY

First published in Great Britain 2004

Copyright © 2003 by SLOANE TANEN
Photographs copyright © 2003 by STEFAN HAGEN

The moral right of the author has been asserted

Bloomsbury Publishing Plc, 38 Soho Square, London WID 3HB

A CIP catalogue record is available from the British Library

ISBN 0 7475 7074 4

2 4 6 8 10 9 7 5 3

Design by MATT LENNING

Printed by South China Printing Co. Ltd, Hong Kong/China

for Tracy James
and Amy Scheibe

Maude was peeved. Her 3:30 yoga class was full again. Didn't anybody work in this town?

Had Saffron fully grasped the excruciating pains of childbirth she would have insisted on the epidural from the first. Who cared what the midwives would say? Next time, she might even plan a C-section, or just lay an egg like the rest of the girls.

Samantha looked around the playground in amazement.
Her mother had been right. She really *was* the smartest and the prettiest.

A penny here, a penny there. One day Viveca would save
enough to have her hair thermally reconditioned too.

———————

Cinderella didn't really mind being taunted by her stepmother and stepsisters. She knew she was younger and prettier and that it was just a matter of time until that divine prince from the party figured out her shoe size. Besides, tales of her abusive childhood would be such a novelty at the castle.

Bridget had to ask herself if the "all over" body wax had in fact been a very bad idea.

Helen knew all about the dangers of UV rays...but roasted, baked, or fried, she simply looked her best with a tan.

Dorothy couldn't believe she had to stand in line.
Didn't they know who she was?

Of course Mitchell encouraged Caesar's efforts to lose weight, but ever since he'd started the Atkins diet, Caesar's inexplicable mood swings and sweet meat breath had forged a wedge between them. As they lay in bed together not touching, Mitchell wondered if it was all worth it...

Marshall, Will, and Holly quickly realized there was nothing routine about this expedition.

Now well into their forties, the fellas sometimes wondered if they should maybe start focusing on a different career. Noooo way, dude...nooooo way.

Aviva had really enjoyed her upgrade to first class. Particularly delightful was the stewardess's smug swiping of the blue curtain that distinctly separated the preferred customers from the hoi polloi. But alas, as she was carted away with the other plebeians on the airport shuttle, it was the memory of those freshly baked chocolate chip cookies that illuminated her long-held conviction that she would indeed have to marry well.

Coco had explicitly said chocolate cake. Damn you, Mother!!!

Yes, yes! Elvira did like piña coladas and taking walks in the rain.

Barbara, Flo, and Vera had been sitting outside that soda fountain since 1956.
If it happened for Lana, it could happen for them.

A vasectomy was definitely on Mr. Miller's short list of things to do.

Mona had become increasingly irritated with Emily's insistence that Saturday shopping always commence at Hermès. After all, not all the girls had trust funds, and at 33, wasn't it time Emily finally got a job? The girls often discussed what Emily did all week anyway.

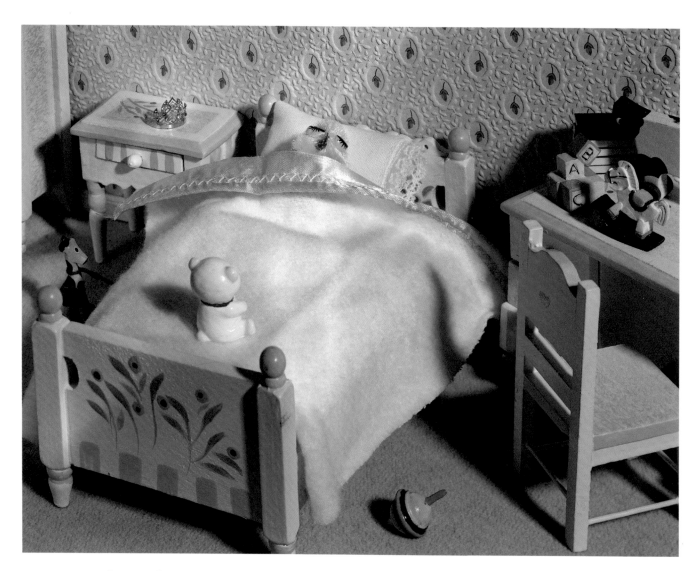

Coco dreamed that one day she would grow up to be a benevolent queen...or a supermodel.

"But you ahh, Blanche, you ahh in that chair."

The Goldbergs really resented this holiday.

Anastasia was through making out with Ian. He was never going to change.

Coco felt her mother's weekly massage was a fantastic opportunity to catch up on quality time.

Jay knew this script would sell. It was hot. Goodbye public transit, hello Ferrari.
Goodbye wife and kids, HELLO Laura Dern.

The Fenwick children had come home with lice...AGAIN.

An eerie silence quickly enveloped the Cohen family wagon. That last turn had been a grave mistake. They were no longer en route to California but heading south, deep into the heart of Kentucky.

Ned was the only one who thought to look up...

On this, their fortieth-wedding-anniversary vacation, it looked as if
both Mr. and Mrs. Prescott were finally going to get what they really wanted.

They called her fat, but Mama called her sturdy.
They called her obstinate, but Mama called her ambitious.
They said she wasn't graceful, but Mama said she was
a powerhouse. And now the hefty little underdog from
Keene Valley had won the gold. The only obstacle
left was getting out of the arena without being tarred and
feathered by Russia and Finland. Mama?

Mary Katherine blamed it on Mary Margaret and Mary Margaret said it was
Mary Josephine. All Sister Agnes knew was that one of the girls was going down.

Abandoned once again in his padded bunker, Jonas plotted a swift and sweet revenge. "Sleep with one eye open, Mother."

Carol was from conservative New England stock, which maybe explained her reluctance to attend a swingers' key party with her husband Bob. But as the couples sat around getting better acquainted, Carol became less concerned with Bob and more intrigued by the possibility that she and Alice's scrumptious Diego might get to take a ride together. Vroom indeed!

Now and again, Cinderella took a ride through the old neighborhood after a day of shopping. She felt it was important to keep in touch with the common folk.

Nipsey's bad manners left Coco speechless.

Princess Gwyneth had her money on Puff.

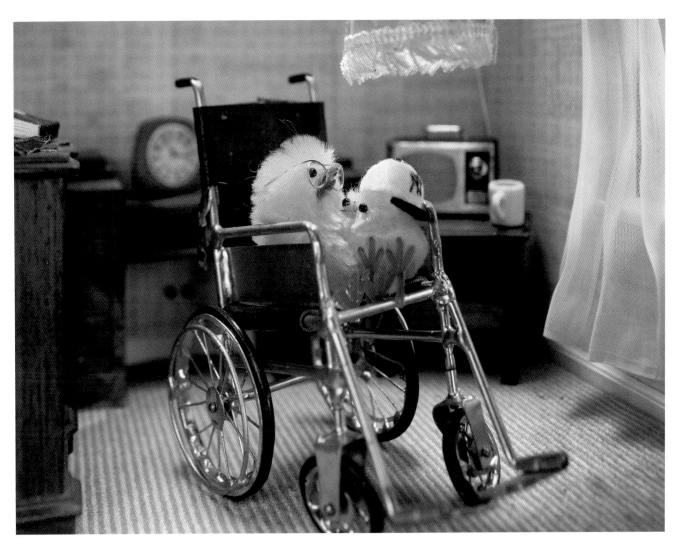

"Back in my day we didn't ask which came first.
There was a chicken, there was an egg, and that was good enough for us."

Caroline's eggs hadn't even hatched and already Victor's eyes were wandering.

Suzanne marveled at the fact that she was still single. Well, at least she had her vintage
Judy Blume collection to keep her company on those long winter nights.

The ladies laughed and laughed and laughed.
Now that would fix Rapunzel's wagon.

Coco was taken aback – she had never seen anything quite so lovely.

At seven, many thought the twins were too old to be breast-feeding. But Mama loved her boys.

朋友们，我们终于到达了！！我们艰苦漫长的旅途终于完了！！
纽约！！纽约！！我们会到高峰，
成为顶尖之王。现在就让我们一起唱，一再地唱！！

Minerva liked to stay indoors where the rooms smelled reassuringly of kasha.
The one time she had ventured out it was chilly and honestly quite frightening.

Paige was devastated to learn that Sarah Lawrence was not one of the Seven Sisters.
So what was the $90,000 for? Her first lesbian experience?

What was he working toward? Dr. Obispo wasn't quite sure...but he was getting there.

The prince's perverse fantasies were beginning to take their toll on Cinderella. Oh well, back to Barneys.

———————

Caitlin had memorized all her lines on the bus ride in from Weehawken. She felt she was a shoo-in. But as she surveyed her competition, her anxiety level reached a fever pitch. Not only was she not the most beautiful girl in the room, she wasn't even pink.

Rambling Rosa

Carl wasn't exactly what Mindy was hoping for...but he *was* Jewish.

The tabloids reported that Cinderella had let herself go since the wedding.

"Ooooooooh!"

Weather, schmeather. It looked like a rowdy bunch and Bea wasn't getting on.

"You binge, I'll purge."

Although Ed and Ted were born Siamese twins,
regrettably, their tastes in television programming had always differed.

At $150 a session, Amy didn't want to talk about her intimacy issues. She wanted to know what Dr. Arlow thought of her new shoes, if he liked the bangs, and whether he too looked forward to their weekly sessions with a gnawing anticipation.

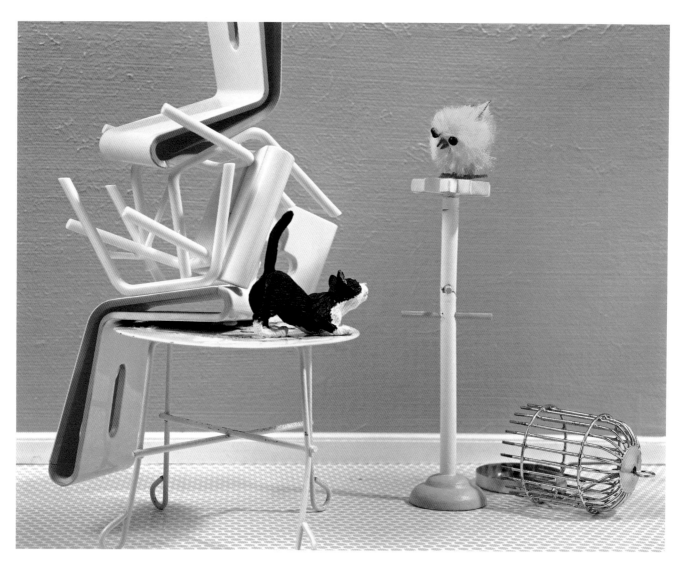

"For the love of God, man, stop calling me Tweety. The name's Nigel."

"Enough with the bread crumbs already. Who's still eating carbs?"

"Yo nasty homey
Don't call me chick
Me and my boyz
Is called the Sniff and Lick

We ain't no gaggle
We the mighty pack
You smooth my feathas,
I scratch your back

Yes I'm the breast meat chicken
Of the doggy ditch
And I'm the lady dog
But don't you call me bitch."

Reuben soon realized that the "family picnic" was just another of his parents' schemes to trick him into exercising. As they finally neared the picnic table he felt he couldn't be held responsible for what might happen if there wasn't a Twinkie in that basket.

ACKNOWLEDGMENTS

Special thanks to Amy Williams for making this project happen, to Stefan Hagen for the beautiful photographs, and to Colin Dickerman, Greg Villepique, and everyone at Bloomsbury for all of their enthusiasm and hard work. I also need to extend my gratitude to Keith Grayhorse for his craftsmanship, Matt Lenning for the design, and Alpesh Patel for always asking how he could help. Finally, I'd like to thank my family: Gary, for putting up with a year of chicken talk, Kitty and Larry for their endless support, Coco for her inspiration; and especially my dad, Ned, for just about everything.

Santantha looked around the playground in amazement. Her mother had been right. She really was the smartest and the prettiest.

Aviva had really enjoyed her upgrade to first class. Particularly delightful was the steward's smug swiping of the blue curtain, definitively separating the male cabin from those preferred customers in first class. As she waited with the hoi polloi for the airport shuttle, however, it was the memory of those freshly baked chocolate chip cookies that illuminated her long-held conviction that she would indeed have to marry well.

Jay knew this script would sell. It was hot. Goodbye public transit, hello Ferrari. Goodbye wife and kids, HELLO Laura Dern.

Maude was peeved. Her 3:30 yoga class was full again. Didn't anybody work in this town?

Marshall, Will and Holly quickly realized that there was nothing about this expedition.

Yes, yes! Elvira did like Pina Coladas and taking walks in the rain.

Yes, yes! Elvira did like Pina Colada and taking walks in the rain.

Ciel wasn't exactly what Mindy was hoping for... but he was Jewish.

Although Ted and Ed were born Siamese twins, their TV-prefer regrettably, had always been different.

Although Ed and Ted were born Siamese twins, regrettably, their tastes in television programming had always differed.

At seven, many thought the twins were too old to be breast-feeding. But Mamma loved her boys.

Desperado, you better let somebody love you...

Page was devastated to learn that Sarah Lawrence was one of the Seven Sisters. So what was the $90,000 for? Her first lesbian experience?

Happy Birthday

Coco had explicitly said chocolate cake. Damn you Mother!!!

Mary Katherine blamed it on Mary-Margaret and Mary-Margaret said it was Mary-Josephine. All Sister Agnes knew was that one of the girls was going down.